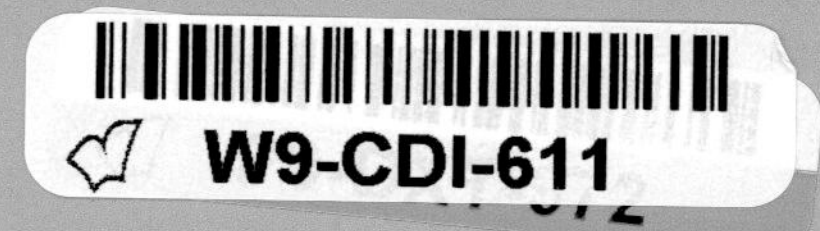
W9-CDI-611

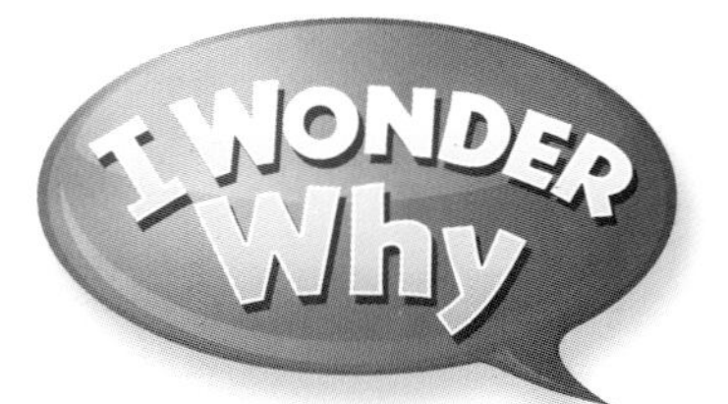

The Earth Shakes

KINGFISHER
NEW YORK

Published in the United States by Kingfisher,
175 Fifth Ave., New York, NY 10010
Kingfisher is an imprint of Macmillan Children's Books, London.

Written and designed by Dynamo Ltd.

Distributed in the U.S. and Canada by Macmillan,
175 Fifth Ave., New York, NY 10010

Library of Congress Cataloging-in-Publication data has been applied for.

ISBN 978-0-7534-7005-3

Kingfisher books are available for special promotions and premiums. For details contact:
Special Markets Department, Macmillan, 175 Fifth Ave., New York, NY 10010.

For more information, please visit www.kingfisherbooks.com

Printed in China
9 8 7 6 5 4 3 2 1
1TR/0612/HH/-/140MA

Contents

What is Earth made of?

The rocky surface of Earth—the part that we live on—is called the crust. Underneath the crust, there is a thick layer called the mantle, made of hot rock.

The core (the middle) of Earth is made of incredibly hot metal.

The Earth

- The core of Earth is superhot. It is about 150 times hotter than the hottest summer's day.
- Deep inside the mantle, rock gets so hot that it melts. It is like gooey caramel.
- This melted rock is called magma.

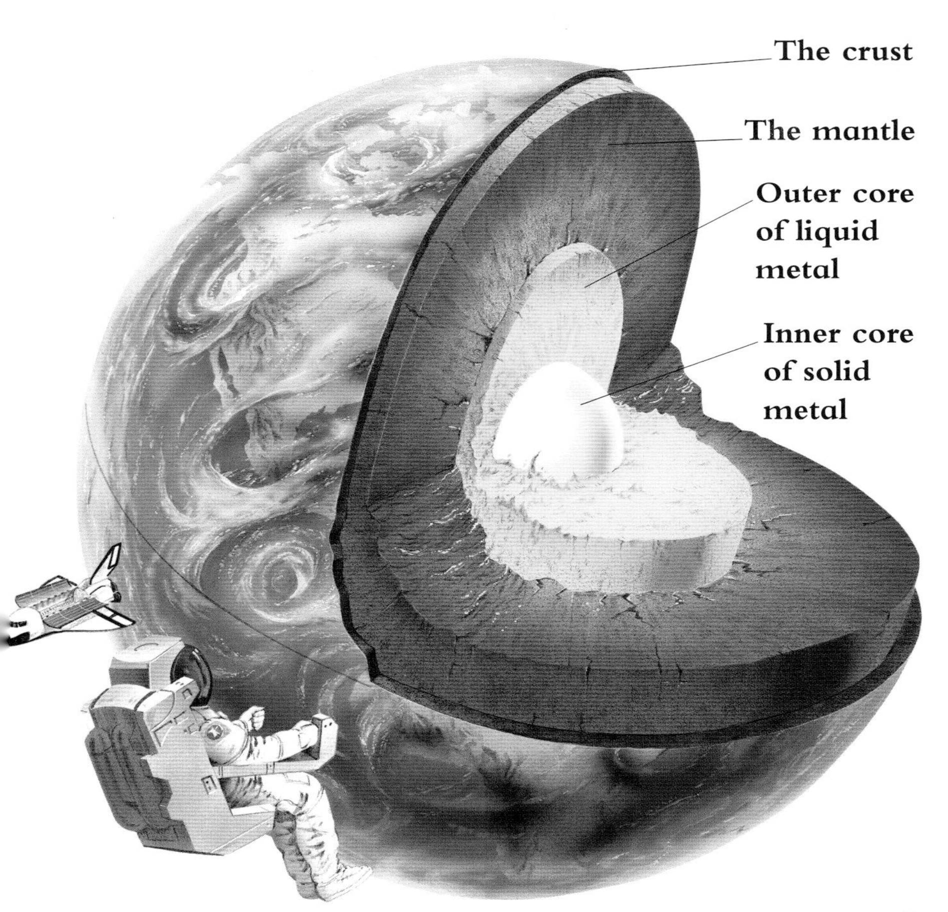
The crust
The mantle
Outer core of liquid metal
Inner core of solid metal

How is Earth like a jigsaw puzzle?

Earth's land is split into seven giant pieces called continents. About 200 million years ago, they were all joined together.

The continents slowly broke up and drifted apart, eventually reaching where they are today.

All about continents

- The continents are still moving—very slowly.
- North America and Europe move apart about 1.5 inches (4 centimeters) each year.
- Asia is the biggest continent and has the most people living on it, too.

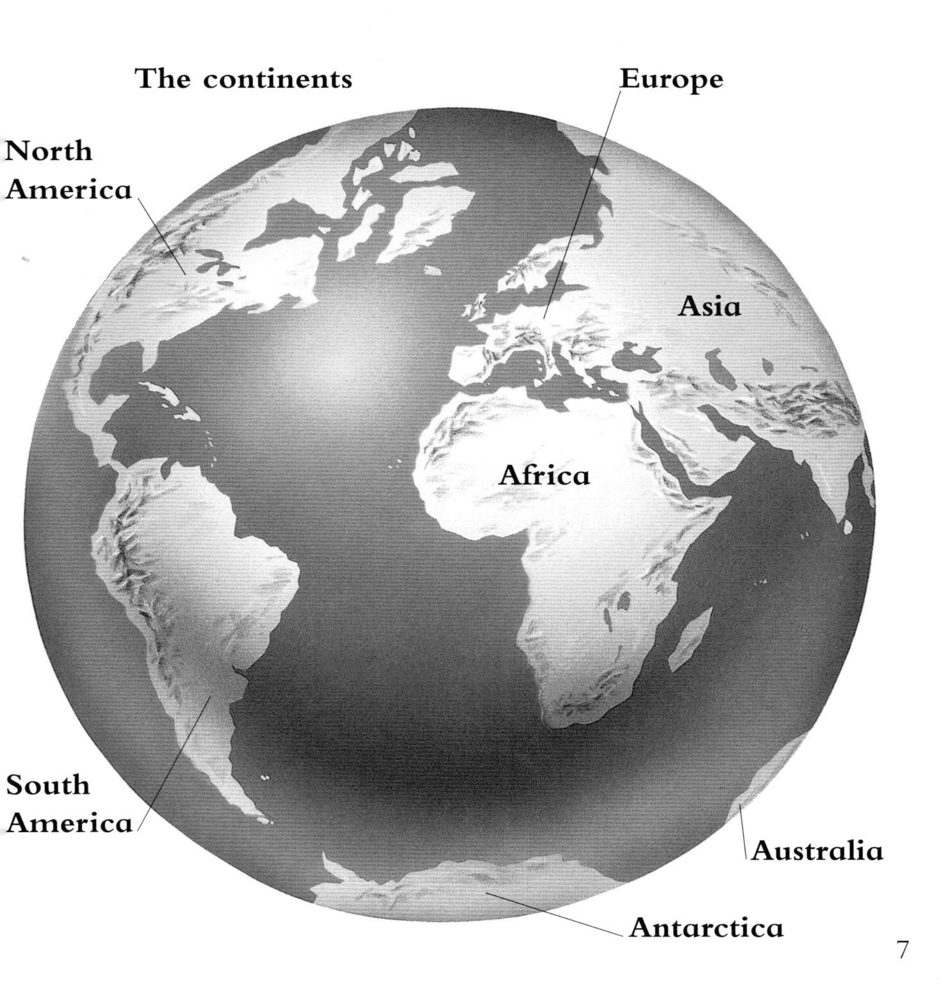
The continents
Europe
North America
Asia
Africa
South America
Australia
Antarctica

Where is the roof of the world?

The Himalayas in Asia are the world's highest mountains. They are in a big group called a mountain range.

The Himalayas are so high that they are sometimes called the roof of the world.

Mountains

- The higher up a mountain you go, the colder it gets.
- High mountains are covered in snow and ice.
- The word *Himalaya* means "home of the snows."

The world's highest mountain is Mount Everest in the Himalayas

It is very hard to climb Mount Everest because of its icy weather

Why do some mountains explode?

Some mountains are volcanoes that can erupt (blow their tops).

Deep inside a volcano, there is a huge chamber filled with magma (hot, melted rock). Sometimes the chamber gets so full that the magma blasts upward. Magma that comes out of a volcano is called lava.

All about volcanoes

- Volcano lava is much hotter than the hottest oven.
- Lava can flow faster than a person can run.
- Hot rocks and clouds of ash fly out of an exploding volcano, too.

Inside a volcano

Lava explodes out of the volcano

A chamber full of melted rock

When does the earth shake?

Earth's surface is cracked into gigantic chunks of hard rock called plates. They float on the hot, runny rock beneath them.

Sometimes the plates push and shove against each other. This is when an earthquake happens.

Earthquakes

- Scientists who study earthquakes are called seismologists (size-mol-o-jists).
- Seismologists try to figure out where and when earthquakes are going to happen.
- Earthquakes don't always happen on land. They often happen under the oceans.

A small earthquake
will make the
ground shake

A large earthquake
can make the
ground crack open

Where are rivers born?

Rivers start out as tiny streams. They bubble out of the ground or are born when ice melts on the side of a mountain.

Streams flow downhill and join together with other streams to become a river.

Rivers

- The world's longest river is the Nile River in Egypt. It flows for 4,150 mi. (6,670km).
- The world's shortest river is the D river in Oregon. It flows for just 120 ft. (37m).
- A curve in a river is called a meander (me-an-der).

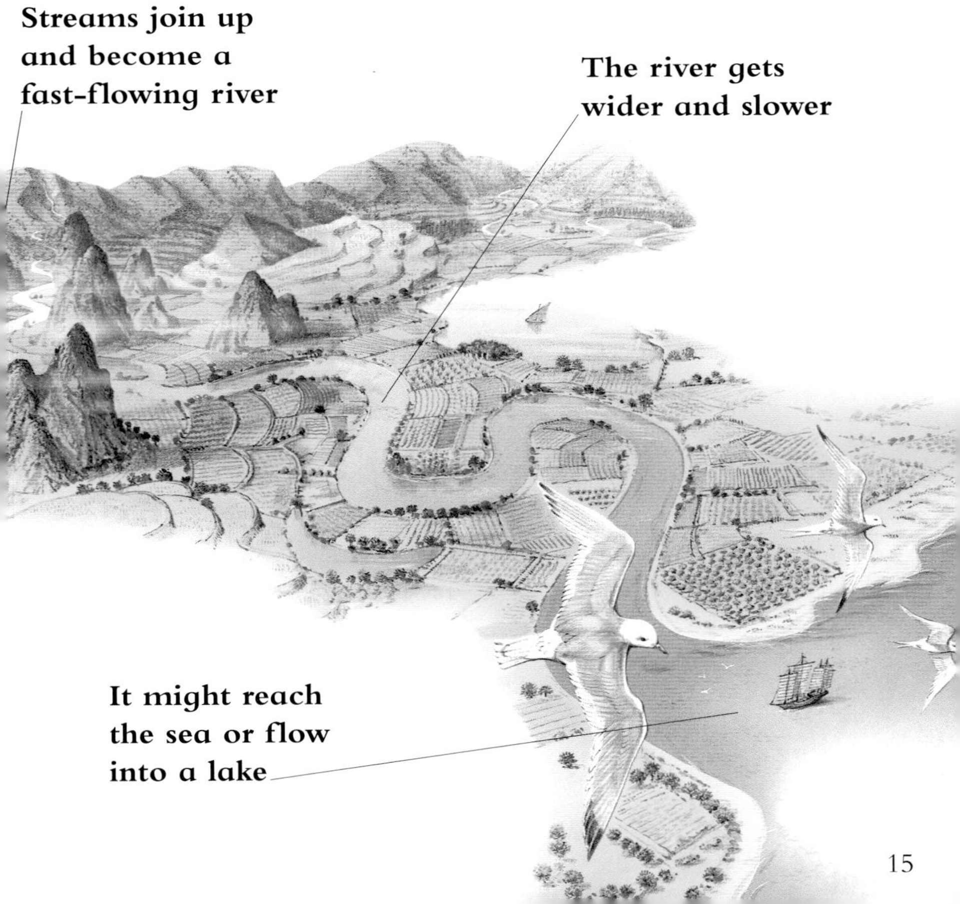

Streams join up and become a fast-flowing river

The river gets wider and slower

It might reach the sea or flow into a lake

Where can you swim underground?

When rainwater trickles underground, it can carve out caves from the rock.

Sometimes the caves are filled with water. Cave explorers called spelunkers ("spill-unk-ers") swim through them.

All about caves

- Stalactites and stalagmites take thousands of years to grow.
- Several caves and tunnels that are linked together are called a cave system.
- Some cave systems are huge, stretching for many miles.

Spikes of rock called stalactites hang down in caves

Spikes of rock called stalagmites grow up from the cave floor

They are made by water dripping off the cave walls or roof

Where are there hills made of sand?

Deserts are the driest places in the world. In sandy deserts, the wind piles the sand up into hills called dunes.

The Sahara Desert in North Africa is the world's biggest hot desert. Large parts of it are covered with sand dunes.

Very few plants can
live in a sandy desert
such as the Sahara

Only a few animals,
such as camels,
can survive there

Where does the sea freeze?

The far north and south of Earth are freezing cold places. They are so chilly that the ocean freezes over in winter there.

When the frozen ocean begins to thaw in the spring, it breaks into chunks called ice floes.

Coldest places

- The far north of the world is called the Arctic.
- The far south of the world is called Antarctica.
- In much of Antarctica, it is so cold that the ice never melts.

Polar bears live in the Arctic, in the far north of the world

They walk over the frozen ocean or swim around the ice floes

What do you know about Earth?

You can find all of the answers to these questions in this book.

Do you think the middle of the Earth is very hot or very cold?

What is the name of the world's highest mountain?

What is lava? Is it hot, runny rock or hot, runny mud?

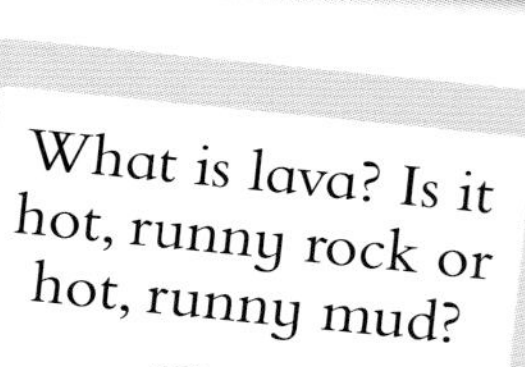

Do rivers flow downhill or uphill?

Where would you find a stalactite or a stalagmite?

Would you like to climb a mountain, explore a cave, or sail down a river?

Some Earth words

Continent A giant area of land. There are seven continents in the world.

Core The middle of Earth.

Crust The rocky surface of Earth.

Ice floe A chunk of frozen sea.

Magma Very hot, runny rock, like gooey caramel.

Mantle A very thick layer of hot rock deep under Earth's surface.

Plate A part of Earth's surface, which is cracked into many plates.